AGE-LONG QUESTIONS

AGE-LONG QUESTIONS

*An examination of certain problems in the
Philosophy of Religion*

by

T. C. HAMMOND, M.A., T.C.D.

Principal of Moore Theological College, Sydney

Foreword by

THE ARCHBISHOP OF SYDNEY

MARSHALL, MORGAN & SCOTT, LTD.
LONDON :: EDINBURGH

MARSHALL, MORGAN & SCOTT, LTD.
LONDON :: EDINBURGH

U.S.A.
ZONDERVAN PUBLISHING HOUSE
815 FRANKLIN STREET
GRAND RAPIDS
MICHIGAN

CANADA
EVANGELICAL PUBLISHERS
366 BAY STREET
TORONTO

MADE AND PRINTED IN GREAT BRITAIN BY PURNELL AND SONS, LTD.
PAULTON (SOMERSET) AND LONDON

FOREWORD

I AM glad of the opportunity of commending the following Lectures to the attention of the reading public.

They were delivered to attentive audiences in the Cathedral Church in Sydney, and I believe they are a real contribution to serious thought on vital subjects.

Canon Hammond is a brilliant scholar of Dublin University, and, as a recent article by him in *The Evangelical Quarterly* shows, is not only a diligent and painstaking student, but a careful and reliable writer.

He has given close attention to the great problems associated in English thought with the name of Bishop Butler. There is always something suggestive and stimulating in his presentation, and I anticipate with confidence that a wide circle will read this present volume.

The course of Lectures herein contained was delivered at the request of the Trustees of the

vi   FOREWORD

Gunther Memorial Fund, which provides that
a series of lectures shall be given at stated
intervals in St. Andrew's Cathedral, Sydney,
in memory of the services rendered to the
Diocese of Sydney by the late Ven. Arch-
deacon J. W. Gunther.

HOWARD SYDNEY.

PREFACE

Butler's *Analogy of Religion* was published in the year 1736. In commemoration of this event, the lecturer contributed an article to *The Evangelical Quarterly*, which appeared in the issue of October, 1936. The subsequent pages may be regarded as an extension of the position there adopted.

The lecturer is glad of the opportunity of laying a small wreath on the grave of a great man.

T.C.H.

CONTENTS

CONTENTS

I

THE PROBLEM OF IMMORTALITY—DO MEN LIVE AFTER DEATH?

MAY I express my appreciation of the honour that has been done me in appointing me to deliver the Gunther Lectures. It so happens that a little more than 200 years ago, one of the most distinguished advocates of apologetics in the Church of England published his famous work on *The Analogy of Religion Natural and Revealed to the Constitution and Course of Nature*. It occurred to me, when I was invited to deal with some aspect of the philosophy of religion, that it might serve a useful purpose if we inquired how far the findings of a distinguished divine, so far removed from the present environment and modes of thought, could still find acceptance at the hands of those who are interested in the graver problems of philosophy and life. Bishop Butler had to deal in his day with the people known as Deists. He broke a lance with Hobbes, whose name is still recognized as a leader in questions relating to social order. He also entered the lists against Shaftesbury, one of the fathers of the æsthetic philosophical outlook upon life and morals.

Much water has flowed under the bridge since Butler's day, and in recent times too little value has been attached to his pronouncements. I cannot but feel that this is a mistake. The thirst for novelty, unduly developed, is shutting off from the modern world much that is valuable in the findings of the past, and we are tempted to believe that this new era, which has been ushered in by the war, has rendered nugatory the wealth of labour and thought expended on foundation problems in the days of our fathers. There is at least danger that this attitude may be adopted without due reflection, and as a consequence, valuable avenues of investigation may be arbitrarily closed against modern adventurers. It does us good to look back upon the past, and it sometimes comes as a shock to us to discover that our grave problems, which are assumed to be the product of advancing civilization, were met and effectively solved in days remote from present experience. Sometimes it is only phraseology that changes. The cardinal facts of life are permanent, and even the expression of them has a certain measure of sameness. This becomes evident once the ancient periods are rendered in the elastic speech of the modern man.

With this object in view, I have selected certain problems that present themselves in the writings of Bishop Joseph Butler, and propose to ask, and in some small measure to answer, the question, What is the relation of these problems to our position to-day? Has Butler offered any solution that might prove of help to a modern inquirer?

The problem that has been chosen for investigation to-day is the problem of personal immortality. It has been conceded that the chapter on immortality in Butler's work is one of the weakest in the whole of his series. If he has a message for our modern times here, a message that transcends the peculiar form of his argument, then it is likely that he will have something of profit to say concerning every other topic that we have selected for discussion. Butler seeks to meet the objection of his opponents that death is the end of all things. He argues that the presumption of death being the destruction of living beings must go upon the supposition that they are compounded, and so discerptible. He opposes to this view of the situation the fact that consciousness is one and indivisible. With the caution which characterizes his investigation, he admits that the simplicity of a living agent cannot be proved by experimental observations, but that these observations fall in with the supposition of this unity. It has been pointed out often enough, and great emphasis was laid on the fact by Kant, that the weakness in Butler's argument here, is that he is contrasting two different modes of existence.

He assumes that because decomposition is the resultant of the failure of living energy in material bodies, therefore decomposition is the only possible means of destruction. Kant suggested, with singular acuteness, that just as air grows thinner in quantity while remaining uniform in bulk, filling a particular space, so the soul of the living being, though one and indivisible, might perish through a form of evanescence. Other critics have urged that any attempt to relate the phenomenon of mind to the phenomenon of extension is doomed to failure, because the method of comparison is inadequate. Matter and mind are disparate, and all that Butler has succeeded in establishing is that a vital force, whatever it may be, is not subject to the laws of extension. We are unable to describe the soul as blue, and hence we regard any analogy drawn from colour as wholly out of place in our attempt to define the reality of our inner being. It is equally futile to say that the soul, because it is not extended, is immortal.

All these arguments have a certain measure of weight, and nobody would confidently urge the plea, that because we are unable to watch the gradual diminution of that to which the term diminution does not properly apply, we are compelled to assume that it must continue to exist. Butler has not given sufficient attention to the very close union that subsists between mind and body, and has not addressed himself to the real crux of the problem. The mind functions, so far as we can observe, only through the powers of the body or the brain. What reason have we for thinking that when the only function of which we are aware ceases, there is a continuance of that power which is no longer evident? The argument for immortality cannot be sustained by any material analogy, and this much may readily be conceded to modern critics.

To come to closer terms with his argument, it might be pointed out that there is a serious defect in his plea that we are capable of utilizing foreign material to supply the lack of some bodily organ. Since his day, immense strides have been made in providing people with artificial limbs, but there is a limit which Butler does not seem to appreciate. Glasses can enable people to see more perfectly, but no invention can take the place of a destroyed optic nerve. In relation to material organization, there is a law which seems to say, "Thus far shalt thou go and no further." It is probably this fact which accounts for the strange incapacity, sometimes met with in men of science, to distinguish between the mental apprehension of sensation, and the actual physical reactions in the organism upon which, in our present condition, it depends. The advances made in biological psychology have not tended to remove these difficulties. But when all these things are said, it simply means that we are asking Butler to leap the centuries and meet, not only the arguments of his own day, based upon the knowledge which was then possessed, but to go further and anticipate alike the discoveries and the objections of a more sophisticated period.

B

Butler, we may argue, met and vanquished the enemies of animism in his day. They chose to adopt a line of crude materialism. They contended that dissolution as such was sufficient evidence of mental destruction. Butler was abundantly justified in pointing out to them that the base of their argument was essentially unsound. May we not attribute to his robust common sense the ingenious speculation of Kant, to which reference has already been made? No doubt Butler was not alone in suggesting the difficulty that arose when attention is directed to the unity of a living agent, but it remains to his credit that he set forth the argument in clear and forcible English, that gripped and held the attention of his countrymen.

But our present object is not to enter a defence of Butler in relation to the circumstances of his time, but to ask a more pertinent question, Is there anything in the argument that still endures? We venture to say that there is. It is to his everlasting credit that he perceived the gulf which separates the physical from the mental. He saw the fact in an age when the empiricism of Locke was powerfully germinating in the mind of David Hume. Hume's *Treatise on Human Nature* saw the light two years after the appearance of Butler's argument. It might be said that the general trend of popular opinion set steadily against Butler's conception, yet he had the courage to express it, and the gift to enforce it. And it is open to us to urge that, notwithstanding the many defects in presentation, the laurels have finally lain with Butler in the controversy. There is an increasing conviction that the chasm between matter and mind has not yet been bridged. Attention is not sufficiently directed to the fact that Butler's argument is negative rather than positive. He is not setting out to establish the actual fact of immortality, he is obviating an objection drawn from the investigations and experiences of his own day.

Allowing him this reasonable interpretation of his effort, we can say that he has set a problem that occupies the attention of scientists in the present day. It is still true to declare

that nothing of material importance has been
added to the argument of Professor Tyndal,
that appeared in the *Athenæum* for Aug. 29th,
1868. Addressing the Physical Science Section
of the British Association at Norwich, Professor
Tyndal said: "Associated with this wonderful
mechanism of the animal body, we have phenomena no less certain than those of physics,
but between which and the mechanism we
discern no necessary connexion. A man, for
example can say, *I feel, I think, I love*; but
how does *consciousness* infuse itself into the
problem? The human brain is said to be the
organ of thought and feeling: when we are
hurt, the brain feels it; when we ponder, it is
the brain that thinks; when our passions or
affections are excited, it is through the instrumentality of the brain. Let us endeavour to
be a little more precise here. I hardly imagine
that any profound scientific thinker, who has
reflected upon the subject, exists, who would
not admit the extreme probability of the
hypothesis, that for every fact of conscious-

ness, whether in the domain of sense, of thought, or of emotion, a certain definite molecular condition is set up in the brain; that this relation of physics to consciousness is invariable; so that given the state of the brain, the corresponding thought or feeling might be inferred; or given the thought or feeling, the corresponding state of the brain might be inferred? But how inferred? It is at bottom not a case of logical inference at all, but of empirical association. You may reply that many of the inferences of science are of this character, the inference, for example, that an electric current of a given direction will deflect a magnetic needle in a definite way; but the cases differ in this, that the passage from the current to the needle, if not demonstrable, is thinkable, and that we entertain no doubt as to the final mechanical solution of the problem; but the passage from the physics of the brain to the corresponding facts of consciousness is unthinkable. Granted that a definite thought and a definite molecular action in the brain occur simultaneously; we do not possess the intellectual organ, nor apparently any rudiment of the organ, which would enable us to pass, by a process of reasoning, from the one phenomenon to the other. They appear together, but we do not know why. Were our minds and senses so expanded, strengthened, and illuminated, as to enable us to see and feel the very molecules of the brain; were we capable of following all their motions, all their grouping, all their electric discharges, if such there be; and were we intimately acquainted with the corresponding states of thought and feeling, we should probably be as far as ever from the solution of the problem. How are these physical processes connected with the facts of consciousness? The chasm between the two classes of phenomena would still remain intellectually impossible. Let the consciousness of *love*, for example, be associated with a right-handed spiral motion of the molecules of the brain, and the consciousness of *hate* with a left-handed spiral motion. We should then know when we love that the motion is in one direction, and when we hate that the motion is in the other, but the 'Why?' would still remain unanswered. In affirming that the growth of the body is mechanical, and that thought, as exercised by us, has its correlative in the physics of the brain, I think the position of the 'materialist' is stated as far as that position is a tenable one. I think the materialist will be able finally to maintain this position against all attacks; but I do not think as the human mind is at present constituted, that he can pass beyond it. I do not think he is entitled to say that his molecular grouping and his molecular motions explain everything. In reality they explain nothing. The utmost he can affirm is the association of two classes of ignorance. The problem of the connexion of body and soul is as insoluble in its modern form as it was in the pre-scientific ages. Phosphorus is known to enter into the composition of the human brain, and a courageous writer has exclaimed in his trenchant German, '*Ohne*

Phosphor   Kein   Gedanke' ('Without   Phosphorus No Thought'). That may or may not
be the case; but even if we knew it to be the
case, the knowledge would not lighten our
darkness.   On both sides of the zone here
assigned to the materialist he is equally help-
less. If you ask him whence is this 'matter'
of which we have been discoursing, who or
what divided it into molecules, who or what
impressed upon them this necessity of running
into organic forms, he has no answer. Science
also is mute in reply to these questions. But
if the materialist is confounded and science
is dumb, who else is entitled to answer? To
whom has the secret been revealed? Let us
lower our heads and acknowledge our ignorance
one and all. Perhaps the mystery may resolve
itself into knowledge at some future day."

When we examine Professor Tyndal's argument, we see that it bears a striking resemblance to Butler's theory that the simplicity
and absolute oneness of a living agent cannot
be properly proved by experimental observa-

tion. However close the association between mind and body, the uniqueness of mental experience continually obtrudes itself. The problem that is set us, as Butler saw, is the union of two disparates, which seems at first sight a contradiction in terms.

But we can pursue the argument somewhat farther, and point out to the objector to mental reality, that ultimately it is the only reality we know. The whole of science is a mental interpretation of what are assumed to be existent facts. Berkeley employed this argument attractively, although defects in his presentation can readily be pointed out. It seems an inversion of the true proceeding to disparage the only instrument by which knowledge is secured, and yet if we are tied up to a material interpretation of the universe, this is the only course open to us. At a much later stage in investigation, Lord Balfour repeated the judgment of Professor Tyndal in a slightly different form. He points out in his *Foundations of Belief* that even if we were able to determine all the vast relations within the wide compass of our knowledge, one problem would still remain for solution, knowledge itself would have to be explained.

What is the strange link that enables man to penetrate into the secrets of nature by employing principles that belong in character to his own inner experience? Why should a world into which the individual enters respond in every portion to the inquiries addressed to it by the individual? We talk easily about investigation by trial and error, but we miss the major problem. Why should investigation yield any reasonable answer at all? To deny it would be to jettison the patient labour of many generations, and resign ourselves to a world of illusion. And yet to assert it is to declare with emphasis afresh the judgment of the Latin poet, Virgil, "Mind moves the mass." Butler recalls us, even though it be in the phraseology of the eighteenth century, to this intimate problem, and it is surely significant that it still demands closer scientific consideration. We are no nearer, says Professor Tyndal in the nineteenth century. Knowledge itself still awaits explanation, says Lord Balfour in the twentieth century.

When we pass from the particular form of the argument to the underlying reality, we are confronted with the fact that thought is sui-generis. No doubt many who earnestly maintain that the soul survives death, do not realize that the same line of argument must compel them to assert that the soul is independent of birth. Leibnitz, indeed, perceived the difficulty, and propounded the interesting question that birth and death were, as it were, retardations and expansions of the real entity, which was something different from the confused experiences to which we gave those names. But there is little evidence that Butler interested himself in the speculations of Leibnitz, probably he would say of the mas of many other problems which did cross his vision, "We have not faculties for this kind of speculation." Nevertheless, he seized upon the uniqueness of the inner experience which we call thought, and demonstrated that it rose superior to matter, and must be granted a measure of independence.

Modern speculation has carried us further along that line, and men are increasingly disinclined to trammel spirit in the trappings of matter. The wave of materialistic philosophy, which produced such an eminent exponent as Herbert Spencer, has gradually retreated. Its best advocates, like the English philosopher whom we have mentioned, were deeply sensible that they had not altogether eliminated the possibility of spirit. They were content, in the language of Matthew Arnold, to postulate at least "A stream or tendency making for righteousness." But it is not too much to say that the hopes engendered of a satisfactory materialistic interpretation even of the sensible world have more and more declined. "Give me," said Herbert Spencer, "matter and motion, and I will make for you a world." A critic bitingly retorted, "Yes, a world of matter and motion." But both matter and motion have been subjected to close scrutiny and analysis in recent years, and the result has been to vindicate once again the supremacy of mind.

It may not be, and we do not think it is, a satisfactory hope of immortality to suggest that such words as dissolution have at best a metaphorical meaning in the region of thought, but it flings the door wide open to higher reaches of speculation, and the robust common sense of Butler would, we are confident, be well satisfied with this result. If we find within ourselves that principle which alone supplies a key to the universe of being, which alone gives meaning to the ordered relation that we call the world, it is difficult to believe that a power so great should perish miserably through the mere accident of matter. If we are not "cabined, cribbed, confined" within the narrow limits of our earthly bodies, then we may claim liberty to give our thought wing, and to entertain those higher possibilities which have ever emerged in the history of man. We can add to the negative argument that asserts that mind has its own laws and therefore must not be restricted within the laws of matter, those other considerations which, from time to time, have arrested the attention of thoughtful men. There is the argument of the unsatisfied longing of the human soul, the persistent battle against extinction which has won at least a temporary triumph, signalized by Horace when he said, "I shall not all die, the greater part of me shall survive the tomb." Man has discovered a means by which he can render his thought durable. We are reading to-day the grandiose descriptions of the ancient monarchs of Babylon and Egypt. By a few skilful marks upon soft clay which is afterwards hardened in the fire, they have defeated the great enemy, and rendered at least their achievements relatively immortal. This is part of man's travail, as well as a wonderful exhibition of his achievement. Death appears as the deadly enemy. To pass out into the unknown is the last grave calamity that can descend upon the human spirit.

It may reasonably be said that unsatisfied desire is too common to enable us to build with any security upon such a foundation. But we are not building entirely upon unsatisfied desire. We are searching for a similar phenomenon here to that which presents itself in nature, and in our thought nature is purposive. We have long abandoned the wild idea of Huxley that man ascended in the scale of being from the amoeba through the greater ape by a series of lucky chances, comparable to the enterprise of an individual who kills a hare by letting off a dozen rounds from a machine gun. There is too much purpose to permit us any longer to entertain an extravagance of this nature. But if purpose displays itself everywhere, what is the purpose of these yearnings after a wider experience that cannot be realized within the compass of an earthly life? And further, it is not straining the limits of our thought to point out that if, wherever we go in the universe, mind is there before us, then the development of mind is the climax

of creation. Personality gives the key to the
universe, and personality refuses to abandon
itself to the night in which all cows are black.
And the fact that time and space are but
elements through which personality rears its
fabric, encourages us to believe that the inde-
cerptibility of the soul, about which Butler
wrote in somewhat hesitating phrase, contains
in it the real secret of being.

It is fashionable in certain quarters to speak
of the littleness of man, and the greatness of
material space, and this reflection is salutary
up to a point. But man reflects again that,
small as he may appear before the lofty moun-
tains, and unutterably insignificant in view of
the great orbs that roll through space, there is
resident in him that one power that alone
discovered this very relation in space. It is
he who gives meaning to the ordered universe
of being. Then man lifts his head again, and
exclaims, "By virtue of what I think I am
great, with a greatness that has in it a promise
of eternity."

II

THE PROBLEM OF SIN—HAS MAN FALLEN?

On this urgent question there is much of interest in the writing of Bishop Butler. The nineteenth century witnessed a period of high optimism on the part of scientific students. There was much to encourage it. Amazing advances had been made in material affairs, and it was not unnatural that men should gain hope from the wide avenues of opportunity that stood revealed as the result of their investigations.

A particular theory of evolution dominated the whole scientific world. Its fundamental thesis was expressed in the lines of Tennyson:

" Arise and fly
The reeling Faun, the sensual feast;
Move upward, working out the beast,
And let the ape and tiger die."

Its hope was in an upward movement which slowly but surely would destroy the inhibitions and retardations that were the consequence of our caveman inheritance. Herbert Spencer was the great prophet of the new era. He looked back on a long period of human history, and thought he traced in it definite stages in moral progress. He looked forward to a complete emancipation from all fettering bonds, including what he regarded as relics of superstition in our Christian faith.

Butler utters a distinct negative to this optimistic mood. His utterances are tinged with deep pessimism. "We are," he writes, "an inferior part of the creation of God." He is deeply conscious of the irrational element which appears as a frustrating influence on high endeavour. It might appear at first sight as if the gloom of Butler had been adequately dispelled in the sunshine of high hope in which the nineteenth-century scientists basked. But the satisfaction which the dawn of a new era introduced failed to capture com-

pletely the thought of its own time. Schopenhauer and Von Hartmann revived in their own
way the old Buddhist longing for Nirvana,
and looked with a degree of despair on the
achievement of mankind. The restlessness of
will was at once for them fascinating and disintegrating. They questioned the value of existence itself, and wondered why this sore travail
had been given to the sons of men.

It is not necessary for us to pursue the
inquiry into this modern phase of pessimism
in order to realize that the problem which our
ancient philosopher set still abides. Here, as
in his excursions into the question of immortality, Butler has still a message for our age.

There are some points in Butler's presentation that call for consideration. His statement
of the condition of the world as he saw it,
bears striking resemblance to what we observe
all round us. He tells us, for example, that
men "appear to be blinded and deceived by
inordinate passion in their worldly concerns
as much as in religion. Others are not deceived,

but, as it were, forcibly carried away by the like passions against their better judgment." He sees in the world an immense moral waste, which issues in "the present and future ruin of so many moral agents by themselves, i.e. by vice." "Mankind," he assures us, "are corrupt and depraved in their moral character." "Revelation," he adds, "supposes the world to be in a state of ruin (a supposition which seems the very ground of the Christian dispensation, and which, if not provable by reason, yet is in no wise contrary to it)". He reaches, indeed, a depth of pessimism when he tells ns, "Whoever will consider the manifold miseries and the extreme wickedness of the world, that the best have great wrongnesses within themselves, which they complain of an endeavour to amend; but that the generality grow more profligate and corrupt with age; that heathen moralists thought the present state to be a state of punishment; and what might be added, that the earth our habitation, has the appearance of being a ruin; whoever, I say,

will consider all these and some other obvious
things, will think he has little reason to object
against the Scripture account that mankind
is in a state of degradation." This is a declara-
tion concerning the facts of experience which,
as the ancient sage himself recognized, offered
no solution to the problem presented.

Perhaps we do well to pause here and learn
a lesson from the method pursued in the
Analogy. Butler does not start, as so many
modern writers seem to do, with an ingenious
philosophy that seeks to explain away the facts
of experience ¡before these facts are duly
appraised. On the contrary, he sets himself
the severe task of outlining the actual conditions in which humanity finds itself, before
he tries to advance any opinion, either as to
their explanation or their remedy. Whoever
adopts this particular mode of investigation
must find himself very largely in harmony
with the judgment that we have described as
pessimistic. Huxley, who cannot be tabled
as a partial witness in matters affecting Chris-

tian revelation, approaches Butler's thought in his own way. He tells us in his interesting Essay on *Evolution and Ethics* : " Social progress means a checking of the cosmic process at every step and the substitution for it of another which may be called the ethical process . . . the ethical progress of society depends not on imitating the cosmic process, still less in running away from it, but in combating it." No doubt criticism may be urged against this violent separation of the cosmic process from the ethical, and cautious theists have rather endeavoured to bridge the gap which Huxley has made. But Huxley was in earnest with his problem. He returns to it again in what Gwatkin calls his grand picture of nature playing chess with youth, "She never overlooks a mistake; but she is absolutely just. To the winner the stakes are paid with overflowing liberality, while the unsuccessful player is checkmated without haste and without remorse." (*The Knowledge of God*, p. 85.) From such presentations we gather at least that

Nature presents to us a relentless movement against the unfortunate—"Nature red in tooth and claw with ravin" marks our delinquencies and offers no hope of redress. This is very far removed from the cheery hopefulness that at one time formed a staple of evolutionary ethics. We are forced to consider that Butler has for his support at least the mature judgment of patient investigators in the field of science.

When we lift our eyes to the theatre of man's actions we cannot lightly dismiss the picture which Butler presents. In spite of all our boasted advance, it is still true that "Man's inhumanity to man makes countless thousands mourn." It is idle for us to talk loftily of the evanescence of evil when the very foundations of our civilization are threatened by the unbridled lusts and ambitions of men. If we were to exclude from our consideration all thoughts of Christian redemption, there seems no justification for the hope that sometime or other the progress of evil will receive a sudden and complete check.

Yet there is another side to the picture, and a side which Butler indicates with great clearness. If we may refer again to Gwatkin, in his comment on Huxley, he draws attention to the words, "without haste and without remorse" and contrasts Huxley's presentation with that of the Prophet Nahum, who tells us, "The Lord is slow to anger and great in power," while asserting as strongly as Huxley that nature has no forgiveness. Gwatkin says: "Where Huxley tells us that Nature checkmates without haste and without remorse, Nahum says the Lord is slow to anger. May not this be true? The long delay is not uncommon: may it not admit a possibility of something better? On the plane of Nature this is pure speculation: Yet I see nothing to forbid it. May there not be mercy somewhere after all? Though Nature's laws roll onward in their unrelenting sequences beyond the reach of mortal ken, there may still be forgiveness in some higher sphere; and by forgiveness I mean no rolling back that car of Juggernaut, as if the word of Nature could be broken in the world of Nature, but the triumph over it of the living spirit which exults in suffering and laughs at death for love and right, serene and calm in sure and certain hope to see and to share an everlasting victory" (*The Knowledge of God*, p. 86). Butler, indeed, is not at the moment calling the resources of revelation to his aid, though he does so in the second part of the *Analogy* to some extent. He is asking the pertinent questions: What is the significance of the long delay in punishment? Does it indicate a probation that could in certain circumstances result in a more favourable issue, even in the case of fallen man?

In his endeavour to come to close quarters with a problem such as this he offers for our consideration two features in nature itself, and then invites us to consider the additional light cast on these remedial indications by the great fact of revelation. Butler here passes from the fact of corruption to a suggested explanation, which has evoked considerable criticism both favourable and unfavourable. As a final solution of the problem of the existence of evil, we are compelled to admit that the suggestion now brought before us is unsatisfactory. As a psychological indication of the manner in which men fall under the impulses that lead to that general wrongness which Butler deplores, there is much in it to excite our admiration. Briefly stated, the argument runs somewhat like this: The immediate object of any given desire is the satisfaction of a particular need. Hunger impels a man to take food. Sudden anger, as Butler develops more largely in his sermons, is really a primitive instinct towards self-preservation. These various qualities or characteristics, by whatever name they may be called (Butler himself prefers the title propensions) seek immediate gratification. But it is the character of ordered conduct to relate these immediate instincts, many of them of an animal nature, to the wide vision of life which presents itself to the personality. The satisfaction of hunger, for example, may be checked from religious or political motives. A man may be content to endure the pangs that witness to an immediate need in order to secure some greater, but more remote, advantage. As a consequence, conflict may arise between the immediate satisfaction and the remote but supposedly higher advantage. The pangs of hunger, to continue our illustration, remain, notwithstanding the lofty conceptions which may animate us. As Butler puts it: "Particular propensions, from their very nature must be felt, the objects of them being present; though they cannot be gratified at all or not with the allowance of the moral principle. But if they can be gratified without its allowance, or by contradicting it, then they must be conceived to have some tendency, in how low a degree soever, yet some tendency, to induce persons to such forbidden gratification." It may come as a surprise to some students of our modern textbooks to realize that observations of this kind are common alike to Joseph Butler in the eighteenth century, and to Jonathan

Edwards, a late contemporary. It warns us that our alleged advances are often more imaginary than real. What Butler calls propensions, and deals with more directly in relation to natural appetites, James, the Harvard psychologist, calls impulses, and reminds us that "when any emotional state whatever is upon us, the tendency is for no images but such as are congruous with it to come up. If others by chance offer themselves they are instantly smothered and crowded out." So that here the observations of the Bishop find re-enforcement from an acknowledged leader of at least one school of modern psychologists. The impulse which demands immediate satisfaction clouds the reason. The higher instincts, even the higher advantages, are neglected in favour of a present pressing necessity. We are reminded again of Butler's observation, similar to that which has been quoted earlier, that men "are so taken up with present gratifications as to have in a manner no feeling of consequence, no regard to their future ease or fortune in this life, any more than to their happiness in another."

We may acknowledge the acuteness of the psychological observation without committing ourselves to the theory that it offers as the solution of the Fall. According to Butler, our propensions have a tendency to break out in any direction, and he regards this as evidence of a measure of instability in our constitution. A severe critic might retort upon him that he has substituted the fact for an explanation of the fact. It is no doubt true that the reason man "breaks out" is because he is under the influence of a specific desire. "An impulse" in the language of James, clouds his better judgment, but the moment that his judgment is clouded he has already over-balanced. What we want to discover is how the harmony which ought to characterize his inner being has been disturbed. If men were originally constituted with reason dominant, and all their desires brought under the control of this higher principle, how did the rebel overthrow the government?

Along this line it may be said that Butler's natural explanation misses the mark at the final point of consideration. The mystery of evil and the reality of the Fall carry us into a region where speculation ultimately fails. Augustine saw that long ago when he pointed out that the mistake which men made in endeavouring to resolve the difficulty is the mistake of explaining the irrational by means of the rational. So far as we know, no modern psychologist has come any nearer than Butler to the solution of the problem of man's defiance of sound sense and judgment.

But when all this has been said, the constitution of human nature does, as Butler contends, render man a very suitable object for probation. If we are permitted to indulge in the speculation that moral determination, as distinct from mere natural conformity to rectitude, involves a deliberate act of choice on the part of the individual, and that such choice produces inevitably a fixed character for good or evil; then the relation of what Butler calls our propensions to what ought to be the higher control of reason does offer a very suitable method of placing man on probation. No doubt the rigid idealists would reject with scorn the view that at the beginning of our race man emerged in a condition of innocency and holiness, but with an innocency and holiness which awaited stabilisation in experience. But we must not make ourselves slaves to rigid idealism in this region where human knowledge reaches its limit. If holiness in its ultimate issue means the direct choice by the individual of right in contrast to a possible wrong, there is something of value in an examination into the peculiar constituents of our nature, and we accord Butler the palm for daringly prosecuting this investigation to the extreme bound of limited human vision. No doubt if Butler himself were interrogated on the question he would agree with Barth, at least to the extent of acknowledging that natural theology brings us face to face with a problem which, apart from revelation, must remain insoluble.

The second feature to which Butler draws attention is the well-known influence of habit upon character. We return for a moment to Gwatkin's question, "May there not be mercy somewhere after all?" Notwithstanding the relentlessness of nature, which, without haste and without remorse exacts its full toll of every action, our attention is directed to the fact that discipline produces a fixed resolution towards virtue. The constitution of nature is such that it offers indications that the steady pursuit of the gleam of truth creates in the pursuer an ever-increasing capacity of apprehension. In the Scriptural illustration, "The path of the just is as the shining light, that shineth more and more unto the perfect day." Amid all the disorder of our disordered universe there is a hindering process to the rude march of vice. Reason, though no longer the unquestioned dictator, is seen struggling to assert its authority over even degraded man. It has been discovered by experience that a course of training and education may correct many vicious tendencies even though, as Butler sadly reflects, the majority of men are but slightly influenced in this direction. What Butler asks us to consider in this connection is well worthy of our consideration. Even when vice has secured its victory by dethroning the dominant principle, there remains a witness in nature itself to a higher and better state of things, and there are prudential, as well as higher moral reasons, which impel men along this course.

It has been pointed out that Butler's range of reading was somewhat limited, but it is certain that he drew very largely upon the labours of Aristotle. In this particular argument we find a trace of the old master. The pursuit of the mean, which is in itself a corrective to inordinate desire, presented itself to Greek thought as that which is eminently suitable to rational man. What Butler is striving to impress on his contemporaries is that such a provision offers indication in itself of a final purpose in nature, which, however

D

checked, still displays itself. He is like an excavator, who here and there traces a noble capital, or the line of a fine building, which offer to him indications that at one time a beautiful structure had been in contemplation, but had been destroyed by the ravages of time. Not only may we say "in contemplation", but actually in existence. To Butler, of course, the voice of conscience, with its continual call to a higher duty that men had neglected and despised, offers the strongest confirmation of this final purpose of God. But he shows, and it is worthy of our consideration, that in the sublunary sphere there are still operating principles in nature which find their true explanation in a mind conformed to righteousness. Though these principles have been distorted and defaced to a very large extent, their presence is a witness to higher things, and not only a witness, but a call.

It is perhaps worthy of notice here that Butler, with his robust common sense, points out that nature's gleam is only efficacious when we follow it. He makes the well-known distinction between active and passive habits. Two quotations may help to make clear what he regards as the indication of a higher purpose in nature, and the possibility in some measure of our attaining to it on the natural plane. He says: "Thought and consideration, the voluntary denying ourselves many things which we desire, and a course of behaviour far from being always agreeable to us, are absolutely necessary to our acting even a common decent and common prudent part, so as to pass with any satisfaction through the present world and be received upon any tolerably good terms in it: since this is the case, all presumption against self-denial and attention being necessary to secure our higher interest is removed." But the danger which confronts frail humanity in view of high ideals is clearly expressed in the following sentence: "But going over the theory of virtue in one's thoughts, talking well, and drawing fine pictures of it; this is so far from necessarily or certainly conducing to form a habit of it, in him who thus employs himself, that it may harden the mind in a contrary course, and render it gradually more insensible—i.e., form a habit of insensibility to all moral considerations."

Taking Butler's salutary warning to heart, the earnest traveller on the road to virtue finds the horizon stretching endlessly before him. He may be convinced by experience that there is a goal in view in nature, but there is ever present with him the bitter reflection that nature is thwarted in her pursuit of the goal. To revert to our former illustration, and to alter the metaphor, the lines of a glorious building are unfolded in the philosophy which tells us that the man who governs himself by right reason is the wise man, but neither the apathy of the Epicurean, or the ataraxy of the Stoic have achieved this result. Butler might have borrowed from the Stoic writers his gloomy descriptions of the mass of mankind—indeed he does refer to the Greek moralists who felt this burden pressing heavily upon them. And so we seem to come to a strange impasse. Nature is ever destined to show lineaments of higher and greater things, and never able to complete her picture.

Butler would remind us that the existing limits should set us upon inquiry, and therein he speaks truly. But how shall the picture be painted? The eighteenth-century moralist is not insensible of the urgency of this question. He tells us: "Upright creatures may want to be improved; depraved creatures want to be renewed." Where nature at best points the way with trembling finger—a way which has been blocked to her through the miseries and wickedness of mankind—redemption comes to her aid. The message of the Saviour, "Except a man be born again he cannot see the kingdom of God", reminds us at once of the hopelessness of restoration by our own efforts, seeing that habits are fixed in a wrong direction, and the possibility of such an intervention on the part of the Most High as shall deliver us from the bondage of corruption. Natural theology, with its intimations of holiness and immortality, cries out for such a solution, which falls to be considered in a subsequent lecture, when we hope to deal with the problem of salvation.

III

THE PROBLEM OF PROGRESS—MYSTERIES IN NATURE AND IN GRACE

ONE of the burdens which press upon the thoughtful is the comparatively slow rate of human achievement, and the extraordinary checks which have occurred in the progress of the race. The civilization of Rome, to take a modern instance, almost perished in Europe. Barbarian hordes with a rude civilization occupied territories that had imbibed much of the Roman culture. The very arts of reading and writing, which at one time were almost as common as they are to-day, disappeared in the experience of the vast bulk of the people. Literature suffered a set-back from which it is but slowly recovering. Were it not for the enterprise of the Christian missionaries, who brought at once new ideals and an old culture to bear upon the barbarian masses, the pall of ignorance, superstition, greed and tyranny might still remain unlifted.

Butler, indeed, would remind us that things are as they are, and would deprecate any imaginative excursions into the might-have-been. But it is obvious that there are hindrances to development which constitute serious obstacles to the alleged uniformitarian advance which was extremely popular in the nineteenth century, and is still a fetish in certain quarters. Why should reason continually struggle with the graveclothes of mistake, misplaced desire and short-sighted policy? Why should not the advance of man be steady and uniform, each succeeding age holding in trust the treasures of the past, and making its own contribution to true advancement? The Christian answer is a sufficient answer, "There is sin in the camp." But Butler's Deist opponents refused to acknowledge that sin was wholly crippling. They had a cheap and easy way of meeting their problems, a way which has not yet been entirely discarded. Where they found a fact they often imagined that they had hit upon an explanation. It is so perfectly simple, "The barbarians, you see, had not the advantage of Roman knowledge, and it would be foolish of us to expect them to emulate Roman methods." For the old Deist and for the modern superficial thinker the world is peopled with the cultured and the cultureless, and they rest here as in an ultimate fact. We have interesting studies offered to us of the primitive savage, and the student never asks himself the obvious question, "Ought we to have primitive savages in the twentieth century?" This is not to deny the value of such investigations, it is merely to point out that they leave the ultimate problem severely untouched.

Our ancient philosopher went a little deeper than the surface. He recognized that there was a retardation of reason to which revelation witnessed, and which his opponents strongly denied. For them there was resident in human capacity the remedy for every ill, and the question of the slow progress of humanity made but little impression upon them. Butler is seeking to show that on the analogy of nature there are indications that the movements towards knowledge and virtue may expect to experience severe checks. He asks his critics to study more closely that book of revelation which they acknowledge, and see whether they do not find in it perplexing circumstances that, if they do not explain limitations to advance, at least indicate that such limitations are portion of human experience. Nature is slow-footed, and therefore the assault upon revelation in this direction has had its flank turned.

In dealing with what we may call the mystery of defeated ends, Butler offers certain suggestions which are, we venture to think, still worthy of consideration. He draws attention first to the fact that prodigality in nature does not destroy the idea of ultimate purpose, and from it draws the inference that there may be a purpose in the discipline of virtue, realized in the few, but ineffective in the many. His argument is worth stating in his own words:

"But that the present world does not actually become a state of moral discipline to many, even to the generality—i.e., that they do not improve or grow better in it, cannot be urged as a proof that it was not intended for moral discipline, by any who at all observe the analogy of nature. For, of the numerous seeds of vegetables and bodies of animals which are adapted and put in the way to improve to such a point or state of natural maturity and perfection, we do not see perhaps that one in a million actually does. Far the greatest part of them decay before they are improved to it, and appear to be absolutely destroyed. Yet no one, who does not deny all final causes, will deny that those seeds and bodies which do attain to that point of maturity and perfection, answer the end for which they were really designed by Nature; and therefore that Nature designed them for such perfection." Butler adds that the appearance of such an amazing waste in nature is to us as unaccountable as what is much more terrible, the present and future ruin of so many moral agents by themselves—i.e. by vice.

It is remarkable that many who have discussed this problem, and we fear we have to include in the number Dr. J. H. Bernard, seem to have missed the fact that there are two separate arguments from the analogy in this particular passage. There is the analogy between an appearance of waste which does not destroy evidence of a final purpose, and the analogy between waste in nature and moral waste through vice. Most commentators have been disturbed by the inadequacy of the second analogy. They have argued with great reason that a seed which offers food for a bird, for example, has fulfilled a beneficent purpose, and hence there is no comparison between a variety of ends which are in themselves valuable, and a check upon purpose which issues in complete ruin from which all elements of beneficence must be forthwith withdrawn. It is possible for us to admit the cogency of this criticism, which is only one of many indications that, notwithstanding Professor Henry Drummond's inimitable parables, natural law does not wholly run in the spiritual world. There are new features which must be taken into account that greatly modify the application of principles drawn from the observance of what we in our ignorance call material forces, and those higher principles that govern the spiritual world. But with profound respect to the many critics of eminence who have seen and indicated this weakness in Butler's argument, which applies more forcibly to its presentation by Berkeley, we venture to point out that there is a primary position which is not affected by these considerations.

In a previous lecture we referred to Huxley's extravagant notion that there was as little evidence for design in nature as might be found in the fact that a man firing a million shots from a machine gun in a particular field killed a hare. According to this theory, Huxley might appropriate to himself the story that is told of the first President Roosevelt. It is said that Roosevelt's opponents, recognizing the strength of his personality, succeeded in shelving him for the Presidency by the ingenious expedient of making him Vice-President of the United States. The Vice-President does not stand for election when the Presidency is vacant. But the chance in a million happened. McKinley was assassinated, and Roosevelt became President, an office which carried with it the right of re-election. When he was returned to power by the suffrages of the people, he said laconically to his wife, "You will be glad to hear, my dear, I am no longer an accident." But Butler would indignantly deny that Huxley is an accident, like President Roosevelt before his election. The fact that nature is slow, makes many pauses, and exhibits what appears to be uncertainty, cannot, to his sane judgment, obliterate the fact that a seed has in it, by irreversible law, the capacity of producing a plant. Surely the argument holds that frustration of design, whatever may be its explanation, is no denial of design itself—else why do we speak of frustration?

Therefore, waste in nature simply means that a particular end, and the designed end, if indeed it be not a contradiction to speak of any other kind in the mental region, has not resulted because of divers forces operating against it. That subsidiary and useful purposes may be served by that which has a capacity for an unrealized development, in no way makes against the validity of the main argument. The moral problem of final laws cannot therefore be urged as an argument against the competency of discipline in this life. The marring is complete in some instances. That is all that we can say in relation to the individual who experiences, in Butler's phrase, "utter ruin." But it is a mistake to bring the final mystery of evil unduly into the argument that nature exhibits purpose, and we cannot but think that Butler has been wise in his reserve. There is an analogy, though, as we have indicated above, the analogy is not adequate to all the circumstances that operate in the moral sphere.

Admitting the principle of design in nature, Butler directs our attention to the evidence afforded that our little scene has reference to a much larger plan. It is interesting in this connection to compare Butler's language with the language of Lotze, who develops a somewhat similar position, contending that man is a microcosm of the much larger macrocosm in which he finds himself. Butler dwells at length upon our ignorance, and it must be confessed that here he has a wide field for the exercise of his ingenuity. He shows that we have been very tardy in our researches. Nature has yielded up her secrets reluctantly, and it would appear at times that we have been long in discovering that which, when discovered, seems to be obvious. One interesting point which he urges with great effect, is that causes, in themselves undesirable, have yet in the scheme of things, been directed towards beneficial results. "Many a man would have died had it not been for the gout or a fever; yet it would be thought madness to assert that sickness is a

better or more perfect state than health;
though the like, with regard to the moral
world, has been asserted." Here there is just
a hint that even in the progress of moral ruin
certain beneficial results have been made to
accrue to others through the over-ruling providence of God. We are reminded of the similar
argument of the Psalmist, "Surely the wrath
of man shall praise thee: the remainder of
wrath shalt thou restrain." And we are reminded further that in the view of the Psalmist
and of Butler, the beneficial result has not
been in the end itself, but in those relations
which have been imposed by a superintending
intelligence. It is ignorance of these relations
that should cause us to speak with great
caution concerning the failure of any end either
in nature or grace.

With reference to the tardiness of nature in
revealing to us very necessary matters, Butler
directs our attention to two simple facts.
The capacities for discovering certain secrets
were in the possession of mankind for long

E

years, and yet, as Butler puts it: "How capricious and irregular a way of information, would it be said, is that of *invention*, by means of which nature instructs us in matters of science, and in many things upon which the affairs of the world greatly depend; that a man should by this faculty be made acquainted with a thing in an instant, when perhaps he is thinking of somewhat else which he has in vain been searching after it may be for years."

The second consideration is that remedies and diseases are not experienced concurrently. "Men are naturally liable to diseases, for which God, in His good providence has provided natural remedies. But remedies existing in nature have been unknown to mankind for many ages, are known to but few now; probably many valuable ones are not known yet." So that even potential provision may lie beyond our reach, and for causes which, in our ignorance we are unable fully to understand, may be delayed in their practical application to the needs of mankind.

There is one further consideration which ought to be dear to the heart of the modern scientist. There is a peculiar relation between reason and experience. Reason can only work upon data, and the series of data upon which it works lies at any rate outside the individual. It would carry us far afield to discuss the systems of philosophy connected with the transcendental ego, but on the plane on which Butler operates, and which remains to us as those who are subject to the incidences of phenomena, the argument still holds. If then we are dependent upon a source which presents itself as other to ourselves for the material upon which reason works, this is a striking confirmation of the opening thesis in this argument that "this little scene of human life, in which we are so busily engaged" has "a reference of some sort or other to a much larger plan of things." The details that present themselves for our observation and reflection are but fragments of the great whole. Reason, indeed, has a capacity for leaping beyond the immediately given, and creating some conception of a mighty system in which each part is contributory to a designed end, but frequently after its leap it falls back upon itself, baffled by the complexities of nature, and has to confess in the language of the ancient patriarch, "Lo, these are parts of his ways: but how little a portion is heard of him?"

The question that presents itself in view of this brief synopsis of Butler's argument is concerned with its relation to present-day intellectual advance. Have we surmounted the obstacles with which the eighteenth-century apologist so plentifully strews our path? It will occur at once to the investigator that ignorance is a phase of agnosticism. There is a story told of a conversation between Huxley and the minor poet, Aubrey de Vere. The spiritual pilgrimage of the two men was different. De Vere followed Newman into the fold of the Roman Catholic Church. The conversation to which we have referred ran somewhat as follows: Said Huxley, "De Vere, I have invented a new religion, and I have been at some trouble to get a name for it. You see, those ancient people who called themselves Gnostics, professed to have hold upon secrets of life and experience. I find so many puzzles in nature that I am at the opposite pole. I have decided to call my religion Agnosticism." "Well," said de Vere, "You have, I suppose, a new religion, and you have a new name in Greek. But it is a very old one in Latin, Ignoramus." We can pardon the flippancy when we remember that de Vere loved a joke, but Huxley's name for his new religion has come to stay. It is shouted at us from the very corners of the streets.

We pause for a moment to notice a rather startling inconsistency in most of the disciples of agnosticism. They are very confident that the moral and spiritual world lies somewhere beyond the purview of man's reason. Only that which is the subject of experience, the data, as Butler argues, upon which reason works, can offer any sound basis of knowledge.

But they have an amazing confidence in the progress of science. What ever else may fail, the retort tube delivers its findings with all the authority of infallibility. This has become a popular slogan, and the camp followers of the agnostic leaders almost deafen us with their asseverations that they are approaching nature from the standpoint of science, and calling the Christian God to the bar of human experience. This is not an unusual pheno- menon, but that does not make it any the more reasonable. David Hume, the prince of sceptics, were he alive to-day, would smile grimly at this inversion of what he believed to be the true order of thought.

But all that we need to insist upon is that the extension of the area of practical knowledge has oppressed men with a still deeper sense than formerly of the fact that they are toying with parts of a great whole, a whole which they aver must for ever escape them. And we can go further, and notice that the genuine leaders in the agnostic position have approximated very closely to the argument of Butler. They make a distinction between partial and total ignorance. They are in entire agreement with the old Bishop with reference to his contention that ascertained facts must have their due weight, notwithstanding that they emerge from a mist which no human light can adequately penetrate. Romanes, indeed, is quite explicit in his view as to this service which modern agnosticism has rendered to the Christian faith. In his *Thoughts on Religion*, written after his return from a period of barren scepticism to the spiritual certainty of faith, he writes: "Now all the strongest objections to Christianity have ever been those of the antecedent kind, hence the effect of modern thinking is that of more and more diminishing the purely speculative difficulties, such as that of the incarnation, etc. In other words, the force of Butler's argument about our being incompetent judges, is being more and more increased." Those who resent Romanes' return to the Christian position are fond of suggesting that the explanation of his action is found in a complete breakdown of his mental powers. This has been explicitly denied by his intimates, but fortunately for our position it is not necessary to enter into the controversy, as we find a similar attitude adopted in his earlier work, *Darwin, and After Darwin*, where he states, "Even if a virgin has ever conceived and borne a son, and even if such a fact in the human species has been unique, it would not betoken any breach of physiological continuity." Bishop Gore quotes Huxley as saying: "The mysteries of the Church are child's play compared with the mysteries of nature. The doctrine of the Trinity is not more puzzling than the necessary antinomies of physical speculation; virgin pro-creation and resuscitation from apparent death are ordinary phenomena for the naturalist."

With such support in the range of modern speculation, the cautious utterances of Butler demand a very close attention. So far from modern science contradicting his judgment that our little scene has reference to a much larger plan, the extension of the area of knowledge creates an ever widening horizon, and further suggestions as to the inter-relation of parts in our universe, and the limited measure of the knowledge which we possess.

Even if we are to take the argument that there are diseases that are cures, it finds striking confirmation in the modern conception of the function of bacteria. They are regarded as destructive, after a manner which creates new and superior collocations that would be impossible but for their disintegrating influence. Mr. Drummond, Assistant and Lecturer in Botany, University of Glasgow, informs us: "Ordinary coloured plants all directly or indirectly owe their supply of nitrogen to the activity of Bacteria . . . By the combined action of these different microbes on land and in the sea the supply of nitrates required by green plants is continually replenished." (*Science in Modern Life*. Vol. IV, p. 44.)

Nor can we exclude from our purview Butler's theory of the discipline of vice. In the moral sphere that which is itself evil, being resisted, issues in good to the individual who resists. So the progress of nature exhibits a measure of slowness, due to retarding influences, and even in many cases examples of retrogression. It will be familiar to some of my hearers that Professor Henry Drummond uses this particular form of argument with great effect in his *Natural Law in the Spiritual World*. Too much attention has been paid to this particular treatise, and we feel we must register again our conviction that Drummond's book is more of a parable than a demonstration. He says, for example, that "nature sets her face most sternly against parasitism," and regards the parasite as evading the great law of the struggle for life. This attaches to a lower organism a degree of purpose that would be commendable even in the case of a Professor, and raises the very urgent question as to why, if nature is opposed to deterioration, deterioration as a fact exhibits itself. Butler's argument is not wholly free from this difficulty. Vice is unrelieved defect, and it is not immediately apparent how a defect can become a minister to perfection. But it must be said in justice to him, that he has a firm hold upon the doctrine of divine grace, and while he properly meets his adversaries on their own platform, he would no doubt reply to conjectures of the sort which we have conceived by asserting that vice itself has an altered character to the resister, when a remedial scheme of things has been introduced in the grace and mercy of God.

This brings us to the conclusion of the whole matter. We have to ask ourselves, in view of our partial comprehension of things, Are we ever justified in suggesting that the empirical is the final? If we were to offer a comprehensive criticism of the modern successors to Butler's Deist objectors, we would say that they have become enmeshed in their own net. The indications that nature herself reveals that we are in possession of a very small part of the whole have been steadily ignored. Relations that govern the conditions of progress and retrogression within our limited sphere have been taken as indications of the final solution of the whole matter. Not only so, but in our folly we proceed to cut off the branch on which we sit. We ignore the fact that Hume perceived so clearly, that science is after all but the relation of ideas. Our systematic arrangements would perish utterly did they not find their place in an arranging and comprehending mind. Surely here there is an indication that our little scene, if it bears reference to a much larger plan, can only bear such reference where the larger plan is one of purpose and moral determination. Outside of these qualities, which are the inalienable possession of consciousness, we would indeed be driven, in the language of a German philosopher, into that night wherein all cows are black.

IV

THE PROBLEM OF SALVATION—HOW IS CHRIST THE SAVIOUR?

CERTAIN religious elements belong to man's nature and condition. Up to the present we have been considering the general arguments based on this fact. These belong to the first part of Butler's great treatise, and constitute in their nature a defence of the old view of natural religion, which has been subjected to severe criticism at the hands of Karl Barth. We venture to express the conviction that the positions laid down by Butler have not been overset by any modern reconstruction. There is what the Apostle calls a groping after God, if haply we may find Him, in the natural state of man. The obscuration occasioned by sin, and the consequent extravagances that emerge in the process of groping, cannot destroy the basal experience. A sound reflection will bring us back again to the older conception which has been violently assailed in the interests of transcendentalism, which it by no means impugns.

But Butler carries us farther, and penetrates into the region of revealed religion. Here the form of his inquiry is, Can we discover in the processes of nature similar features to those which display themselves in a revelation from God to man, made in the interests of man's redemption ? In dealing with this aspect of his question, he devotes a chapter to the appointment of a Mediator, and the redemption of the world by Him. Our title to-day brings us to this particular problem. Perhaps there is no aspect of the Christian message that has invited more reflection than this. We are repeatedly told by modern prophets that the whole scheme of mediation is involved in such insuperable difficulties that it can be no longer entertained. Perhaps the shallowest form of modern criticism is found in the assertion that the sufferings of the Son of God involve two grave moral inconsistencies. The innocent is represented as suffering for the guilty, which is a violation of natural justice, and the guilty are set free from the consequences of their sin, which is a violation of moral order. Those who argue after this fashion very frequently add, with merciful inconsistency, that sin can be forgiven, which is to say that merited judgment shall not fall.

If we can discover anything in the natural course of events that offers a parallel to mediation, while the moral problem remains, the weight of the objection does not lie wholly upon the Christian scheme. But it is not necessary for us to postulate a completely satisfactory theory. That may be beyond our powers. As Butler expresses it: "Some have endeavoured to explain the efficacy of what Christ has done and suffered for us, beyond what the Scripture has authorized; others, probably because they could not explain it, have been for taking it away, and confining His office as Redeemer of the world to His instruction, example and government of the church." It is worthy of note that Butler regards the objection which "represents God as being indifferent whether He punished the innocent or the guilty," as extremely slight. He does so because of his contention that it concludes "altogether as much against God's whole original constitution of nature, and the whole daily course of Divine providence in the government of the world—i.e. against the whole scheme of Theism, and the whole notion of religion, as against Christianity." These are bold words, and certainly give pause to those who fancy that objections of this sort have seen the light of day only in our developed modern world. Two hundred years ago they received serious treatment at the hands of a thoughtful divine. It may, perhaps, appear that little can be added on either side to the position then adopted.

Butler's first contention in this interesting chapter is that the general notion of a mediator between God and man is consonant with what we know in nature. He points out that throughout the whole of nature there is a law of mutual dependence. In the words of the Apostle Paul: "None of us liveth to himself, and no man dieth to himself." The appointment of a mediator between God and man rests on the sure base that nature exhibits to us mediators who are instruments of good and evil to us, and as Butler adds, instruments of God's justice and mercy. Our very entrance into life, and our nurture in the early days of our existence, entirely depend on the instrumentality of others. If life itself is mediated, it seems, Butler would argue, an absurdity to deny the principle of mediation. Further, as he is careful to point out, when we accept the possibility of revealed religion we are assuming that the world is under the proper moral government of God. Revealed religion adds to the experiences incidental to our condition by nature the conception that "the consequences of vice shall be misery in some future state, by the righteous judgment of God." There is nothing, he suggests, in this revelation that runs counter

F

to the analogy of earthly experience. Many miseries follow our course of action at present, and are dependent upon the course we take. Poverty, sickness, infirmity, and death at the hands of civil justice, are such consequences. He challenges his Deist opponents to face squarely the problem which they have raised. If we are to deny that sin invites punishment hereafter, because punishment as a natural consequence of sin is inconsistent with experience, then we are forced to reject the whole process of civil justice, and in addition to deny many palpable facts. But the argument that the wicked must not escape the consequences of his wickedness, nor yet the innocent suffer for the guilty, runs equally counter to a thread of mercy discoverable in the constitution of nature. All the bad consequences of our actions are not visited upon us. In many cases through the interposition of others these evil effects are obviated. This, says Butler, may be called "mercy or compassion in the original constitution of the world."

We have more than once had occasion to direct attention to the remarkable caution that signalizes Butler. He rarely, if ever, presses an argument beyond its lawful limits. The same moderation in discussion is observable through the whole extent of this chapter. Butler contends that the analogy of nature or providence to which he has directed attention is not in itself sufficient to create a positive opinion on the matters in dispute. He regards it as offering a sufficient answer to "a mere arbitrary assertion without any kind of evidence." It is interesting to notice that he regards the popular opposition to the mediatorial office, which rests on the indefensibility of the innocent suffering for the guilty, in this light. He contends that there is no evidence whatever for the position thus laid down. Nature offers so many examples of suffering unjustly incurred, that in the light of its evidence the assertion that the innocent do not suffer for the guilty becomes impossible. The question that remains, and with which he attempts to deal, is, Can such a provision of nature be directed towards remedial ends? Can the necessity for the interposition of others, which is a condition of our being, be so directed that sin itself and its consequences may be removed from our path? With the wisdom that characterizes him, he tells us that the proof of such a possibility lies not in reason, but in revelation.

It would seem as if this argument regarding mediation receives additional strength in these modern days. In the world in which we live rapidity of communication is an important feature. Australia is within ten days' reach of Great Britain. Our letters travel to and fro with amazing regularity. The world has been opened up through sea and land routes, so that nations are linked together in a manner that could not be even contemplated in the days of Butler. One consequence of these victories in the realms of time and space has been to make our dependence one upon another even more evident than formerly. If we address ourselves, for example, to the economic problems associ-

ated with the distribution of raw materials,
this fact becomes abundantly evident. Before
the Great War an agitation in Serbia involved
millions in conflict by reason of this inter-
dependence. To-day the armed camps of Europe
give evidence of the same fact. He would be
a bold man who would deny that no man liveth
unto himself, and no man dieth unto himself.
Paul, as well as Butler, holds the truth of the
matter so far as this particular analogy carries
us. Nor if we turn to the more peaceful and
praiseworthy aspects of modern life can we
form any other conclusion. The Carnegie trust
issues its literature to create a sentiment for
world peace. Just in proportion as it exercises
any influence, it illustrates the general principle
of mediation. In fact, so long as men are bound
together by a common bond of reason, and so
long as they are compelled to share mutual
interest and advantages, so long the relation of
man to man will contain in it an element of interposition that affects the fortunes of the individual,
and in some measure regulates his destiny.

Why is it then that an objection which seems to run counter to the whole course of experience still finds its earnest advocates? Butler suggests in reply that the heinousness of sin is scarcely appreciated. Men are sensible that evil consequences follow irregular and disorderly behaviour, and they are prepared to admit that the greater the irregularity, the greater the evil consequences. But there is a realm of offence in which their conscience is blinded. The confusion and misery introduced into the Kingdom of God do not press as directly upon the heart and mind as those lesser evils which are part of our daily experience in the general constitution of things. Yet, says Butler, if we regard these evils by which men blaspheme the Lord of all, and are injurious to their fellow creatures, the creatures of God, in their proper light, it would be impossible for us to say whether, consistently with the eternal rule of right, the consequences of such evils could be prevented: nor are we in a position to say what the unprevented conse-

quences would be. One fact is abundantly
evident: "It is clearly contrary to all our
notions of government, as well as to what is
in fact the general constitution of nature, to
suppose that doing well for the future should
in all cases prevent all the judicial bad consequences of having done evil, or all the punishment annexed to disobedience."

The argument thus far follows two lines,
lines which are apparent in every part of the
Analogy. There is positive evidence that nature
admits of the interposition of individuals who
are not themselves the prime actors in any
drama of good or evil. This interposition is
of two kinds. Men direct retribution so that
it falls upon evildoers. Very many of the consequences of sin are due to the reactions of
society against the sinner. This fact illustrates
the particular subject under review by empha-
sizing what has been called in recent years
"the solidarity of the race." Mackenzie gives
point to some of the conclusions reached by
Butler: "The principles of duty," he says,

"which an individual recognizes are largely determined by the social universe which he inhabits. Hence his conscience also must be largely determined by this. A man's conscience, we may say broadly, attached itself to that system of things which he regards as highest. There is, indeed, a certain feeling of pain, analogous to that of conscience, in connection with every universe in which a man lives, whether he regards it as the highest or not" (*Manual of Ethics*, Book VII, Chap. 1, Par. 14).

This quotation leads us to the second and much more important form of interposition. There are interventions which are morally beneficial. Vice is retarded by positive law, mediated to us often by those who have a better conception of our needs than we have. It is apparent that most of the progress of mankind is due to causes external to the great mass of humanity. Carlyle was certainly not thinking of theological implicates when he wrote that men might well prize their kings or strong men. Yet he was reiterating the argument of Butler. Through the conceptions of others we climb to higher heights of endeavour than any we could reach unaided. Progress is not a straight line. Nor is it the simple evolution of latent concepts. It is conditioned at every stage by the better enlightened who reflect rays of truth that the less fortunate could never otherwise catch. And our modern world is recognizing more clearly a duty to the unfortunate. We are told that we must elevate the masses even at the cost of our own self-indulgence. It is a good principle. But it is the principle of mediation. We bear the burden of the unprofitable. Every argument that suggests that by bearing it we may mitigate or remove it is an argument for mediation. "The quality of mercy is not strained." But mercy is mediation in the garment of compassion. If we cannot lighten by one straw the heavy loads that bear our brethren down, if we cannot wipe away a single tear of the sorrow-stricken, it is idle to talk of mercy. If

we can, then the argument of the old divine
returns with force: "The visible government
which God exercises over the world is by the
instrumentality and mediation of others."

The second argument is developed along
what may be called a negative line. Let it be
conceded that the principle of remedial interposition is part of the law of nature. Let it
be admitted that the social unit directs and
controls the individual unit. Still it does
not follow that we are competent to decide the
exact limits of interposition, nor in any given
instance to determine beforehand the precise
character of the interposition which is effected.
Here, with his robust Anglo-Saxon common-
sense, Butler rules out of discussion problems
regarding the origin and permission of evil.
He is content to take the humbler road of
experience. The Author of Nature permits
evil. "He has provided reliefs, and in many
cases perfect remedies for it, after some pains
and difficulties." He has provided reliefs even
for that evil which is the fruit of our own

misconduct. These reliefs are of two kinds
in the ordinary course of nature. Men can
do much themselves to obviate the consequences of their own rashness or vice. Much
more can be done for them by others. These
things are apparent from the observation of
the general laws of our social life. But they
carry with them certain limitations which we
do well to regard. The very fact that evil
itself is something which is not wholly explic-
able warns us against rash conclusions as to
what may, or may not, be possible in the
matter of deliverance. In the same way we
discover that the interposition of others is
provided to remedy evil, but we do not see
clearly the actual reason for this. According
to Butler, the fact of our unity one with
another, and the consequent result upon our
lives, is much more apparent than the grounds
on which this fact is based. Therefore we are
cautioned that, "Though it is highly right,
and the most pious exercise of our understanding, to inquire with due reverence into the ends

and reasons of God's dispensations, yet when those reasons are concealed, to argue from our ignorance, that such dispensations cannot be from God, is infinitely absurd."

"God instructs us by experience (for it is not reason, but experience which instructs us) what good or bad consequences will follow from our acting in such and such manner: and by this He directs us how to behave ourselves." The light falls upon positive obligation, while the ground and reason often remain to a large extent shrouded in darkness. From this we are counselled to observe very carefully our duty to the revealed Lamb of God. Following the analogy of nature we might conclude that God's part in redemption effected by His Son would be only partially apprehensible. Our part would stand forth as clearly revealed. The divine injunction, "Believe on the Lord Jesus Christ" is within the limits of our capacity and the sphere of our understanding. Even if it were not so, "Surely a divine command is abundantly sufficient to lay us under the strongest obligations to obedience", to the extent of our comprehension of it.

But this argument which deprecates certain conclusions because they are based upon ignorance, must not be confused with the facile modern theory that "the fact of the Atonement is what matters." Butler has a very clear sense of the difference between partial and complete ignorance. He would insist, indeed he does insist in the instance before us, that the plain statements of Scripture should be given their full value, and that no formulation can be regarded as complete which does not include all the relevant statements. His argument is not that we should decline to speculate, but that we should temper our speculations with due regard to our ignorance of final causes. He resembles here the earlier English philosopher Bacon, who cautions us that in theology as in philosophy, "many things must be left abrupt." It is a superficial treatment to equate Butler's argument with any popular modern divorce between theory and fact. Our ignor-

ance, on which he bases this negative conclusion, is ignorance of the precise nature of
punishment in the world to come; the reasons
why its infliction would have been needed;
our ignorance how far anything which we could
do would, alone and of itself, have been effectual
to prevent that punishment.

Further, it is not in our power to determine
the whole nature of our Lord's office as Mediator,
or the several parts of which it consists. It is
obvious that the aim of these cautionary reflec-
tions is to bind us more closely to the revelation of God. Butler would have little sympathy
with those who would seek to substitute for
the express language of revelation some finely
spun theory, based on supposed agreements
with human experience. He would insist that
all such reasonings are vitiated by the obvious
fact that at every step of the inquiry we are
confronted with an impassable barrier—our
own ignorance. His emphatic protest is worth
hearing: "Let reason be kept to: and if any
part of the Scripture account of the redemption

of the world by Christ can be shown to be really contrary to it, let the Scripture, in the name of God, be given up: but let not such poor creatures as we go on objecting against an infinite scheme, that we do not see the necessity or usefulness of all its parts, and call this reasoning; and, which still further heightens the absurdity in the present case, parts which we are not actively concerned in." Indeed, in Butler's explanation of the Scriptural terms descriptive of the Atonement, he exhibits clear evidence of the popular opinions of his age. His view is that the death of our Lord Jesus Christ is a propitiatory sacrifice. On the divine side there is much that has not been revealed as to the rationale of this sacrifice. But it is apparent that through His death our Lord Jesus Christ has placed men "in a capacity of salvation." His death made repentance efficacious, an efficacy which it could not exhibit without it. The existence of sacrifices all over the heathen world is evidence of this conviction that repentance in itself is not sufficient.

Students of historic theology will recognize
at once the type of thought which was opera-
tive largely in the eighteenth century. This
ought to be sufficient to determine the object
of Butler's appeal to our ignorance. He is
precluding a sentimental rejection of the revelation of God's love in the Person of Christ on
grounds which reflect on the whole constitution of nature. Providence has its mysteries
no less than grace. Both are systems partially
revealed.

What then, we may ask, is the final message
which the analogy with nature offers us? It does
not convey to us any inkling of the manner in
which the mercy of God stoops to our low
estate. But when the appointment of a Mediator has been revealed as an act of divine
clemency, it offers parallels that assist our
understanding of the message. Others inter-
vene for our help even when the consequences
of our own ill-doing are in question. Often at
great loss to those others our burden is removed. We, indeed, frequently suffer involun-

tarily for the sins of others, but the sufferings
of Christ were voluntarily endured. The statements of Scripture compel us to believe that
Christ offered Himself by way of satisfaction
for the sins of men. God's providential government exhibits vicarious punishment as an
appointment of everyday experience. This
coincidence between providence and revelation
silences objections, and throws us back in
faith upon the Lamb of God who taketh away
the sin of the world.

V

THE PROBLEM OF EVIDENCE—PROBABILITY THE GUIDE OF LIFE

THE question was asked long ago, "Can a man by searching find out God?" The pursuit of truth is alluring and baffling. Much has been said upon this subject since. But the problem is ever the same and is ever with us. It lies at the root of the modern development in theology associated with the names of Barth and Brunner. They state it in a startling, and what many regard as a one-sided manner. Brunner tells us: "The solution of the puzzle which is in the 'possession' of faith does not amount to 'insight': our vision is not right through, but in 'a dark mirror'; the assertions of faith are one and all paradoxes. The 'natural' man takes offence at them, for they are mysteries in which God reveals Himself as the Incomprehensible. They never become 'illuminating', but all through life remain merely credible, and certain only to faith. We never attain to the tranquillity afforded by sight: that is reserved for eternity. Thus faith itself is not the solution, but faith knows of a future solution which, by the grace of God, shines beforehand into the present. . . . It is knowledge of that event to which revelation points, when partial knowledge will be terminated, and when opposition between reality and truth, between abstract idea and concrete character will cease; and faith can take away the final poignancy of this opposition even now" (*Philosophy of Religion*, p. 96).

Brunner has his special point of view which is not in consideration at the moment. The quotation illustrates the fact that the element of incomprehensibility asserts itself to-day as it did in Butler's time. From a different source in our modern world, we have an echo of this sense of mystery—this revelation that we stretch our hands still towards the unknown. Sir J. Arthur Thomson writes: "We maintain that the world of life is rich in beings and doings, becomings and results, that should fill us with wonder. The basis for this wonder is to be found in certain qualities of organisms which must be at present taken as 'given.' We study fractions of reality, and we are at pains—which are pleasures—to reduce them to common denominators, which enable us to discern unity. But continually we come face to face with what we cannot at present reduce any further. What the future may have in store, no one can tell, we are bound to say *ignoramus*, but never *ignorabimus*; the horizon of science, as some say of the horizon itself, is expanding. But we cannot get scientifically beyond such qualities of organisms as growing, multiplying, developing, varying, unregistering, feeling and endeavouring; and yet they give us a conviction of 'beyondness.' To take account of such facts of life is part of man's normal experience. Their study interests, educates and enriches; it helps to keep alive the sense of wonder which we hold to be one of the saving graces of life. . . . Facing everyday things in the world of life, around which our scientific fingers will not meet, what can we do but repeat what is carved on the lintel of the biology buildings of one of the youngest and strongest of American Universities: 'Open Thou mine eyes that I may behold wondrous things out of Thy Law'" (*The Great Design*, p. 259).

So the philosopher and the scientist meet in declaring that all our great advances have but opened vistas with horizons greatly expanding. "Explanation," said someone, "is the substitution of one great mystery for another." Paul tells us, "The things which are seen are temporal." Butler suggests that "Revelation" (may be) "no more than a small light in the midst of a world greatly overspread, notwithstanding it, with ignorance and darkness." Spencer, in the interests of sense perception, assures us that there "has arisen an awe of Reason which betrays many into the error of supposing its range to be unlimited" (*Principles of Psychology*, Pt. VII, c. 2).

Now the effect of all these statements as to man's final incompetency may be to discourage the adventurer after truth. That inference has been widely drawn in modern days. As long ago as 1877, Professor Flint showed that "Comte's fundamental objection to theism and theology is, that they imply that man can attain to a knowledge of causes, whereas causes are, he holds, absolutely inaccessible to the human intellect" (*Anti-Theistic Theories*, p. 193). It is here that Butler enters with his robust common sense. If the road of investigation is long and weary, it is nevertheless true that it is bordered by precious fruit all along its course. If the ultimate lies still beyond our comprehension, the immediate has practical consequences that ought not, and, in some cases, cannot be ignored. Butler seems to have two great aims in his doctrine of probability. He seeks to check unlicensed speculation. There is a close affinity to earth in his presentation that reminds us of Dr. Johnson's refutation of Berkeley. The seer of the London coffee houses tapped his stick upon the ground. That was to him an ultimatum. Berkeley should retire defeated when threatened with the doctor's stick. In somewhat similar vein, but with more measured speech, Butler warns us against "building a world upon hypothesis like Descartes." There is, indeed, little of the mystic, and very little of the metaphysician about Butler. More than once he bids his imagination, when it would take rein, to "return to this earth our habitation." He demands a basis in fact for every piece of "abstract reasoning" in which the mind indulges.

We can indeed argue from the known to that which is similar, from what is present to "what is likely, credible, or not incredible" in the future. But the hard rock of observed fact must be beneath our feet. This is the negative side of Butler's proposition. Where there is no probability there is no guidance. He is a cautious mariner who declines to hazard his ship in wholly unknown waters. There was need in his day for this caution. We cannot say that the need has disappeared to-day. The Deist of the eighteenth century had undiminished confidence in his own powers. The celebrated Irishman, John Toland, was so far removed from the modern concept of awe in nature that he propounded the view that Christianity was not mysterious. Like most periods of intellectual ferment, high hopes were awakened at that time that the riddle of the universe would be read. Butler comes to an age of self-confidence, and by means of critical analysis shows that we have no faculties for many investigations with which we seek to burden reason. His is the sane outlook which demands due regard to the findings of experience, even when the aim is to transcend experience. He is most particularly anxious to establish the fact that we need a revelation from God to assure us of certain great and important matters which are accepted as commonplace because the source from which they rise is forgotten or denied.

It must be admitted that along this line

Butler rendered signal service to his generation. And we need to reiterate his message to-day as the wisest and best of our true students clearly apprehend. The very restlessness in our persistent search after facts, and ever fresh facts, offers evidence that a vast ocean of the unknown stretches from us to meet the horizon. We journey forward, but only to find an illimitable waste still ahead. And yet, with a singular perversity, there always arises the temptation within us to regard knowledge as closed, and in our superiority to refuse the unusual and the eternal alike. This is the day of so-called "advanced thought." There is a tendency to relegate to the scrapheap much of the lore of the past. We are bidden in certain quarters to adopt "a wise agnosticism." This seems an echo of Butler's negative position. In point of fact it is a direct contradiction of it. Agnosticism, like Butler, professes to keep the solid rock of sense experience beneath its feet. But very daringly, and in a manner wholly foreign to our present guide, it passes to the assertion that sense experience is the whole of reality so far as our power of comprehension carries us.

Butler cherishes no such illusion. He would contend that the very fact of knowledge in itself passes beyond the limits of sense experience. It would be too much to expect him to speak the language of modern scholars. But there are not wanting indications as to where he would place his emphasis. His whole argument on personal identity, at which we glanced in the first lecture of this series, places him unalterably on the side of the idealist in any controversy concerning the relation of impressions to a living agent. Knowledge for him gives meaning to life, and knowledge he possesses. Hence, so far from adopting the agnostic position as that is understood in these times, Butler would reject it. He would hold that it offered an instance of the very defect against which he warns. It is legitimate, indeed, to argue from a part to the whole, if we assure ourselves of the accuracy of observed facts. But agnosticism is arguing that a part is the whole, and erecting thereby false barriers in the path of progress. Butler's thought lends support to Green's dictum, "a consistent sensationalism would be speechless." He would, we are convinced, endorse the dictum of Professor Thomson, "We are bound to say *ignoramus*, but never *ignorabimus*," rather than the counter position of Comte and Schopenhauer, that to the end we must remain ignorant of reality.

But the more important contribution that Butler makes is the positive application of his theory. We are under moral obligation to use the powers that God has given us, even when the light they are able to cast is but a feeble ray. "I express myself with caution," he writes, "lest I should be mistaken to vilify reason; which is indeed the only faculty we have wherewith to judge concerning anything, even revelation itself." A chastened mood that recognises our limitations is far different from a despairing attitude indulged because of them.

"That which is true, must be admitted, though it should show the shortness of our faculties."

This pithy sentence embodies in its short compass the two ideas which govern the whole argument. We can apprehend truth even while we know that the truth we apprehend is but a part of the whole. The urgent claim that is made is that a presumption in favour of a particular attitude of life is often sufficient ground for a course of action. If we were to wait until every difficulty had been resolved we would remain inactive in the face of grave issues, and life itself would become impossible for us. Men in ordinary circumstances take risks. Men act on a definite position even when it is not wholly defined. Total ignorance indeed destroys, or more correctly, precludes all proof and all objections alike. The wholly unknown cannot become an object of the will. But it is otherwise with partial ignorance. Our study of a person's character may enable us to predict with confidence the ends at which he aims. At the same time, our ignorance of his circumstances may leave us largely in ignorance of the best means to attain these ends. In such circumstances we fall back upon the clear evidence of character, and assume that the means are adequate to the end.

Butler's contention regarding the apprehension of truth is most important. At stated periods in history men have been firmly confident of success. Again a period of lassitude and uncertainty supervenes upon their earlier self-assurance. It is difficult to say in what period we find ourselves at present. There are movements towards a great confidence. There are also movements towards dark despair. Between these two there is a mediate position adopted by many, which bids us treasure our instincts towards truth and righteousness, even though they but serve to guide us along the path of our choice, and may be no more valid than other guidances followed by other folk.

Ours is not, on the whole, an age of critical inquiry. Research belongs to the few. Sentiment sways the many. Perhaps it was always so. But the spread of information has at once narrowed and widened the gulf between the critical and the common man. It has narrowed it by bringing a heterogeneous mass of information within the reach of the crowd. It is no longer possible for the scientist to strut on a stage of his own devising, and gaze with contempt on the herd below. Berkeley bids us speak with the vulgar, and think with the wise. But who is wise and who is vulgar? The schools give a smattering of all kinds of knowledge, and the smattering enables the intelligent to speak the foreign language of the technicist. But it has widened the gulf also. The vast accumulation of information demands a life-study from the real man of research. Few have the ability, and perhaps still fewer the opportunity, to devote a lifetime to a particular branch of knowledge. Hence the language of the moderately educated reveals blunders and misjudgments at every point. The wise man sinks into himself and remains "mute while the corypheus spake."

It is not to be wondered at that our modern world has through specialization tended to disintegration. The idea grips the mind forcibly that it is best to regard ourselves as all contributors to an end which is as diverse in form as are the avenues of approach. We do not realize that such an attitude is ultimately a denial of any true end. There is no finality, there is merely process. And at that stage we ask ourselves, Can there be process without finality? So the weary round of human thought repeats itself. Wisdom is found in the play of the Greek Sophist, and the individual becomes answerable to himself, and so answerable to no man.

It is well to be halted by the vigorous thought of two hundred years ago, and challenged as to our position in the face of that which is known. For Butler has a severe seriousness in his determinations. He is not simply satisfying the legitimate aspirations of an acute mind. He is charging upon his hearers a solemn message of responsibility. We cannot, he says,

relieve ourselves of the burden of choice because of the shadows that shroud the beginning and the end of existence. He is in earnest
with his idea, and we are forced to be in
earnest with him. He presses upon his readers
the value of circumstantial evidence. It was
Thoreau who said that circumstantial evidence
may be very convincing, as when a man finds
a trout in the milk. Butler draws attention
to "the importance of collateral things and
even of lesser circumstances in the evidence of
probability." He admits that cumulative
evidence opens itself to easy attack, because
it is easy to raise objections to each particular
item, and to ignore the immense weight of a
mass of coinciding circumstances. Yet he
asserts with confidence that a moral obligation
rests on each reader of the sacred record to
weigh well the circumstances that conspire to
give verisimilitude to the message. If we
needed a warning against superficiality we
have it in this ancient treatise. The treasures
of truth do not unfold themselves to the careless

spectator. That is the burden of his theme. We need to emphasize it in these days when tabloid information has largely depraved the taste for truth.

There is, says Butler, a moral obligation not only to weigh well the circumstances of any message, but to act in accordance with prudence in our relation to the probable. If two courses lie open to us, one of which is attended with risk, and the other free from any dangerous consequences, prudence demands that we should choose the safe path. If there is even a probability that God in His moral government may punish evil, then, in the absence of any evil consequences which may follow attention to this probability, it is our duty to have regard to it. It may seem strange to readers in this century to find a bishop pleading for consideration to revelation solely on the ground that what is presented falls into the category of the possible. But it must be borne in mind that Butler was dealing with a self-confident and aggressive scepticism. It has survived to

H

our day. There was an overweening assurance in the competency of reason. It became necessary to point out that, to quote Bacon again, many things were "left abrupt" in the grandiose argumentation of the day. Butler shrewdly asks his opponents, "Are you quite as sure as you fancy you are?" As in the old days of Socrates a searching inquiry revealed serious gaps in the argument. We know from Hume that the literati of the eighteenth century set light store by Shakespeare. Yet they might have remembered that there are more things in heaven and earth than ever were dreamed of in their philosophy, without much hurt to their pride.

But the proof of ignorance may prove too damning. So it becomes a paramount duty to develop this new argument that there is a duty in regard to probabilities. Because we cannot find out everything, we are not relieved of the task of searching; nor yet of the task of acting, not only on what we discover, but on what appears most reasonable in view of the measure of knowledge which we possess. Those, therefore, who demand full satisfaction of every perplexity before they embrace and obey the manifest declarations of Holy Scripture, are acting contrary to their best interests, and adopting a course that in other departments of knowledge is condemned by the common sense of mankind. Light is shed about our path to enable us to walk. He who stands still and refuses to tread the illumined road because the distant scene remains undisclosed, is guilty of rejecting the aid of the light given.

But there is no connection between the doctrine that probability is the guide of life, as Butler exhibits it, and the doctrine of "Probabilism" which invited the indignation of Pascal. So far from there being any agreement between the two, it would be truer to say that the one is the exact contradiction of the other. Professor Joyce, a recent exponent of Probabilism, defines it as "The moral system according to which, when there are divergent views as to the lawfulness of an action, for each of which solid arguments may be advanced, then, provided the lawfulness be alone in question, we are under no obligation to follow the more probable of the two views, but are equally free to adopt either course. . . . A man is not bound to adopt the more perfect course in all his actions. . . . The study of Christian perfection belongs to ascetical theology." (Art. Probabilism. *Hasting's E. R. & E.*, Vol. x.) Butler is not concerned with two grades of moral conduct, nor would he admit that a higher, when recognized, can be discarded in favour of a lower in any circumstances. He is addressing himself to the much greater problem that all our endeavours are but approximations to truth and reality. He is seeking to disarm the objection that naturally arises from such a contemplation. The shadow lies athwart all our activities. To refuse action because of it would be to condemn the whole human race to complete stagnation. We could not even remain static, for our status would, at any given moment, be as partial and incomplete as any progress we might seek to effect. The alternative which he suggests is the recognition of a moral duty to action. The method which he proposes is a weighing of probabilities. That which is possibly dangerous is to be avoided as definitely as that which is actually found inimical. That which is helpful must be adopted, however many are the questions which still remain unsolved.

He is the prophet of a practical morality which bids us step forth upon the path where the light shines. He would regard the submission to exterior authority involved in the choice of alternatives which Probabilism suggests as a forfeiture of our highest powers. Conscience must be our director. The voice of God within, and not the clamour of voices without, must prove our guide in deciding on which side duty lies. But there must be a devotion to the highest and the best in our determinations, otherwise we have fallen below the high level of moral attainment which God and our conscience demand. The presentation of probabilities may come from without in the ordered principles of society, or in the sacred page of the revealed Word. But the decision comes from within, and can only justify itself by the conviction, "This is best." The issue that confronts us in the light of the evidence available is simply this: Can we act on a portion of truth, or must we wait until everything has been established?

So far is this from being a relic of old-world metaphysics it is pressed upon us to-day with increasing intensity. Lord Balfour expresses his conclusion in "Foundations of Belief" as follows:

"It seems beyond question that any system which, with our present knowledge and, it may be, our existing faculties, we are able to construct must suffer from obscurities, from defects of proof, and from incoherences. Narrow it down to bare science—and no one has seriously proposed to reduce it further— you will still find all three, and in plenty" (p. 355).

The answer which Lord Balfour seeks to give to our question is in part the answer of Butler.

He has indeed a penetrating analysis of the relation of Authority and Reason, which finds no exact counterpart in the earlier writer. But at heart the two investigators, separated by a gap of one hundred and fifty years, have much the same message. Belief, acceptance, have their roots in a sense of need.

The Psalmist, centuries before either, cried out, "My heart and my flesh crieth out for the living God". The soul cannot rest satisfied with the material considerations so constantly pressed upon it. A critical analysis easily reveals that science, with its claim to impartial investigation, bases itself upon age-long reachings after satisfaction. There is an urge towards God, a desire for His manifestation, only met fully by the revelation in Jesus Christ.

INDEX

INDEX

(Books in Italics)